Elizabeth I

Jane Bingham

Heinemann
LIBRARY

www.heinemannlibrary.co.uk
Visit our website to find out more information about **Heinemann** books.

To order:
☎ Phone 44 (0) 1865 888112
📄 Send a fax to 44 (0) 1865 314091
💻 Visit the Heinemann Bookshop at **www.heinemannlibrary.co.uk** to browse our catalogue and order online.

Heinemann Library is an imprint of Capstone Global Library Limited, a company incorporated in England and Wales having its registered office at 7 Pilgrim Street, London, EC4V 6LB – Registered company number: 6695582

Heinemann is a registered trademark of Pearson Education Limited, under licence to Capstone Global Library Limited

Edited by Louise Galpine and Catherine Clarke
Designed by Kimberly R. Miracle, Jennifer Lacki and Betsy Wernert
Original illustrations © Pearson Education Limited
Illustrations by Mapping Specialists
Picture research by Hannah Taylor
Originated by Modern Age
Printed in China by Leo Paper Group

ISBN 978 0 431044 74 3 (hardback)
13 12 11 10 09
10 9 8 7 6 5 4 3 2 1

ISBN 978 0 431044 90 3 (paperback)
14 13 12 11 10
10 9 8 7 6 5 4 3 2 1

British Library Cataloguing in Publication Data
Bingham, Jane
Elizabeth I. – (Levelled Biographies)
942'.055'092
A full catalogue record for this book is available from the British Library.

Acknowledgements
We would like to thank the following for permission to reproduce photographs:
©akg-images pp. 6 (Nimatallah), 11 (Bildarchiv Monheim), 12 (Erich Lessing), 38 (Sotheby's), 39; ©The Art Archive (Palazzo Pitti Florence/Dagli Orti) p. 4; ©The Bridgeman Art Library pp. 7 (Giraudon/ Galleria Nazionale de Capodimonte, Naples, Italy), 8 (Hever Castle Ltd, Kent, UK), 15 (Trustees of the Bedford Estate, Woburn Abbey, UK), 17 (Giraudon/ Prado, Madrid, Spain), 18 (National Portrait Gallery, London, UK), 19 (National Portrait Gallery, London, UK), 21 (Private Collection/The Stapleton Collection), 23 (The Royal Cornwall Museum, Truro, Cornwall, UK), 25 (Private Collection/Richard Philip, London), 27 (Scottish National Portrait Gallery, Edinburgh, Scotland), 29 (Private Collection/The Stapleton Collection), 30 (Woburn Abbey, Bedfordshire, UK), 31 (Private Collection/Rafael Valls Gallery, London, UK), 33 (The Crown Estate), 34 (Private Collection), 35 (British Library, London, UK/British Library Board, all rights reserved), 36 (Guildhall Library, City of London), 37 (Private Collection), 41 (Prado, Madrid, Spain); ©Corbis pp. 16 (Douglas Pearson), 40 (Angelo Hornak); ©National Portrait Gallery (London) p. 32; ©Photolibrary (Robert Harding Picture Library) pp. 9, 20; ©The Royal Collection 2008/Her Majesty Queen Elizabeth II p. 10; ©TopFoto/Roger-Viollet p. 24.

Cover photograph of Queen Elizabeth I in her coronation robes reproduced with permission of ©Corbis (Fine Art Photographic Library).

We would like to thank Nancy Harris for her invaluable help in the preparation of this book.

Every effort has been made to contact copyright holders of material reproduced in this book. Any omissions will be rectified in subsequent printings if notice is given to the publishers.

CONTENTS

Some words are shown in bold, **like this**. You can find out what they mean by looking in the glossary.

ELIZABETH, QUEEN OF ENGLAND

In 1558, a small, red-headed woman was crowned queen of England. She was just 25 years old. Nobody guessed that she would become one of England's greatest rulers.

For the next 45 years, Queen Elizabeth I ruled alone. When she died, England was a peaceful and powerful nation.

This is a portrait of Queen Elizabeth that was painted when she was still alive.

A Tudor queen

Elizabeth was the last of the Tudor rulers. The Tudor family ruled England for more than 100 years.

Henry VII (Elizabeth's grandfather) – ruled 1485–1509

Henry VIII (Elizabeth's father) – ruled 1509–1547

Edward VI (Elizabeth's half-brother) – ruled 1547–1553

Mary I (Elizabeth's half-sister) – ruled 1553–1558

Elizabeth I – ruled 1558–1603

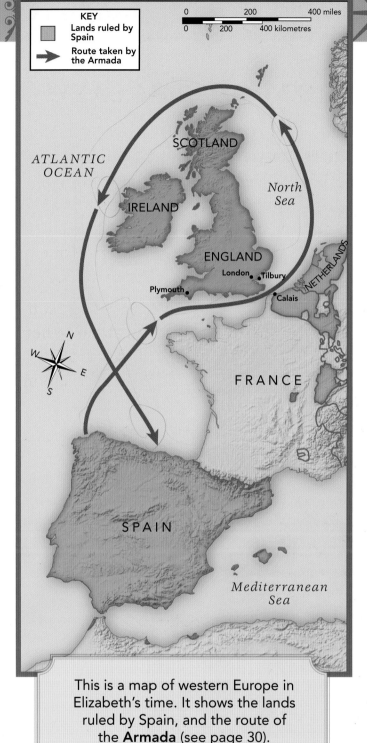

KEY

Lands ruled by Spain

Route taken by the Armada

0   200   400 miles
0   200   400 kilometres

ATLANTIC OCEAN

SCOTLAND

North Sea

IRELAND

ENGLAND

London   Tilbury

Plymouth

Calais

NETHERLANDS

FRANCE

SPAIN

Mediterranean Sea

This is a map of western Europe in Elizabeth's time. It shows the lands ruled by Spain, and the route of the **Armada** (see page 30).

An exciting reign

Elizabeth faced many difficulties. She survived **plots** against her life. She fought off an **invasion** from Spain. She also sent explorers and traders all over the world.

While Queen Elizabeth was on the throne, many people in England became richer. It was also a great time for musicians, artists, and writers. Later, people saw Elizabeth's **reign** as a glorious period in English history. They called this time the Elizabethan age.

A strong woman

Queen Elizabeth never married. She proved that a woman could rule alone. Elizabeth was loved and feared by her people. But most of all she was admired.

KING HENRY'S DAUGHTER

On 7 September 1533, a princess was born. She was the daughter of the king of England, Henry VIII, and his new wife, Anne Boleyn. Her royal parents named their daughter Elizabeth.

A girl, not a boy

When Elizabeth was born, King Henry was very disappointed. He wanted a son to be the next king. At that time, everyone thought that men made better rulers than women. Henry had planned a great celebration to welcome his new son. Now he cancelled all his plans.

This is a portrait of Henry VIII painted in Tudor times.

A second daughter

Elizabeth was Henry's second daughter. Henry had married Catherine of Aragon when he was 18. Catherine had given birth to a daughter, called Mary. Then Catherine had one more daughter, but the baby died. Henry was desperate for a son.

In 1533, Henry **divorced** Catherine of Aragon and married Anne Boleyn. He hoped his new wife would give him the son that he longed for.

Henry's divorce

Henry wanted to divorce Catherine so he could marry again. But divorce was forbidden by the **Catholic Church**. Henry asked the **pope** (the head of the Catholic Church) for special permission. When the pope refused, Henry was furious. He left the Catholic Church and created the **Church of England**. Then he went ahead and divorced Catherine.

In Tudor times, the pope was seen as more powerful than any king. This painting shows Pope Clement VII.

Princess Elizabeth

Elizabeth was sent off to live in the country when she was still a baby. Meanwhile, Henry and Anne stayed in London. After that, Elizabeth rarely saw her parents. She was brought up by **noblewomen**, who dressed her in fine clothes and played with her.

Henry and Anne

Henry had fallen in love with Anne Boleyn when she was a **lady-in-waiting** at the royal **court**. But their marriage was not a success. They both had fiery tempers, and Anne did not give birth to a son. After only three years of marriage, Henry decided it was time for a change. He gave orders for Anne to be **executed**.

Death of a mother

Elizabeth was nearly three years old when Anne was killed. Later, she refused to talk about her mother, but she is thought to have worn a picture of Anne in a special ring.

This is a portrait of Henry's wife (Elizabeth's mother) Anne Boleyn.

King Henry's wives

After Anne Boleyn died, King Henry VIII married four more times. His third wife was Jane Seymour, who died after giving birth to a son. Next, Henry married Anne of Cleves, but he quickly divorced her and married Catherine Howard. In 1542, Henry gave orders for Catherine Howard to be executed. Then he married his last wife, Catherine Parr. Altogether, he had six wives.

Henry VIII caused great resentment by getting rid of the Catholic **monasteries**. The monasteries fell into ruins, and some of them are still ruins today.

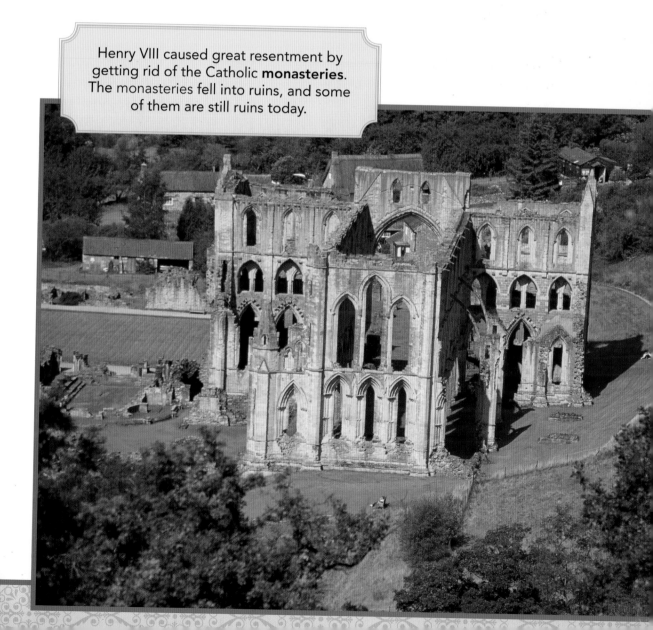

A COUNTRY CHILDHOOD

After Anne Boleyn had been **executed**, Elizabeth was no longer a royal princess. Instead, she was known as Lady Elizabeth. She lived a quiet life in Hatfield House, about 48 kilometres (30 miles) north of London.

Lady Elizabeth

The young Lady Elizabeth had many servants to look after her. She also had a **governess** to give her lessons. As well as learning to read and write, Elizabeth learnt to sing and dance and play music. She spent a lot of time out of doors, riding her horse, and hunting with hawks.

This painting shows Elizabeth when she was about 13 years old.

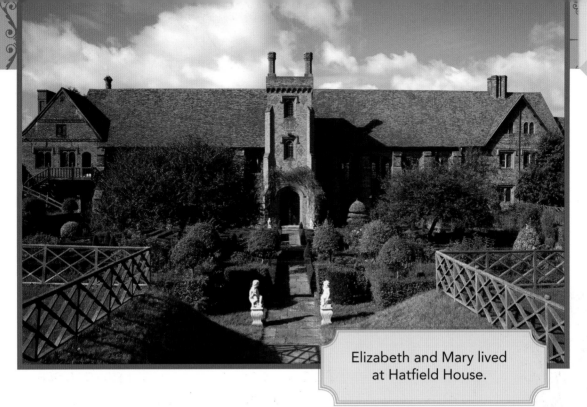

Elizabeth and Mary lived
at Hatfield House.

Mary and Elizabeth

King Henry's oldest daughter, Mary, also lived at Hatfield House. Even though Mary was 13 years older than Elizabeth, the girls were friends. Mary taught Elizabeth to play cards.

Mary and Elizabeth spent a lot of time together, but there was one major difference between them. Mary was a **Catholic** and Elizabeth was a **Protestant** (see box). Many Catholics saw the Protestants as their enemies. Later, this caused serious problems for Elizabeth.

Protestants and Catholics

In the 1500s there were two main religions in Europe: the Catholic Church, which was led by the **pope** in Rome, and the Protestant Church. The Protestants had broken away from the Catholic Church and did not recognize the pope as their leader. Members of King Henry VIII's **Church of England** were Protestants.

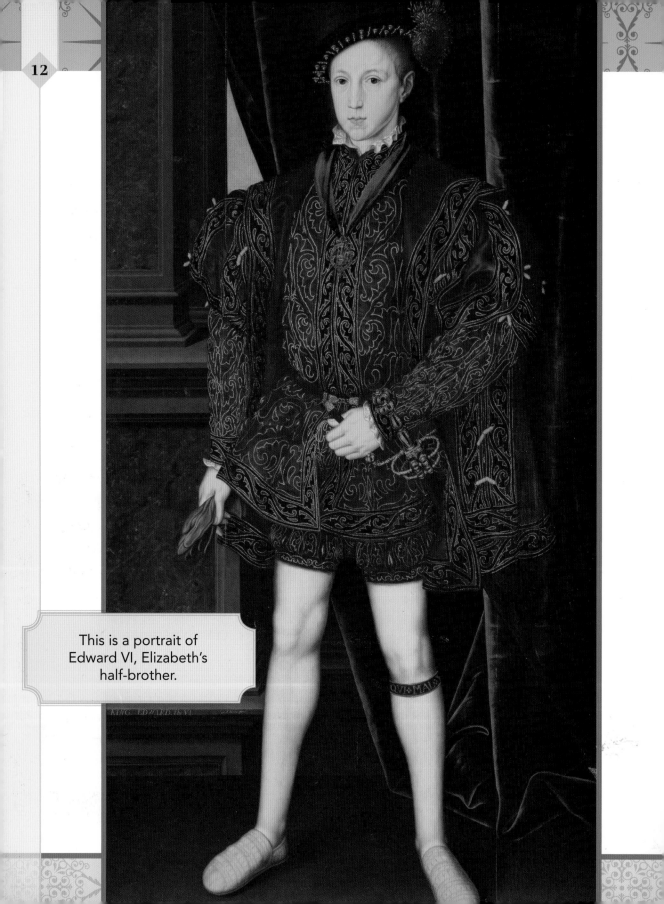

This is a portrait of
Edward VI, Elizabeth's
half-brother.

A prince is born

When Elizabeth was four years old, King Henry finally had a son. His third wife, Jane Seymour, gave birth to Edward. Sadly, Jane died 12 days later. Now Elizabeth was third in line to the throne, behind her younger brother, Edward, and her older sister, Mary. There seemed little chance that she would ever be queen.

Edward and Elizabeth

Elizabeth loved her half-brother Edward. They were both brought up as **Protestants** and they often shared lessons together. Edward was a very clever boy, but he was often ill. He admired his sister Elizabeth very much.

Henry dies

King Henry died in 1547. Elizabeth was 13 years old. When she heard the news, Elizabeth wept briefly, but she quickly recovered.

Elizabeth had never been close to her father because he was always busy at **court**. But in many ways they were alike. Henry and Elizabeth were both strong characters, and they each had a very quick temper. They loved music and dancing, and outdoor sports such as hunting and archery (shooting arrows at targets).

Boys before girls

In Tudor times boys had the right to rule before girls. When a king died, his oldest son was the next in line to the throne. This meant that the oldest son would automatically be the next person to rule the country. If the oldest child in a royal family was a girl, her brother would still rule before her.

ELIZABETH IN DANGER

After King Henry died, nine-year-old Edward became King Edward VI of England. During his **reign** Elizabeth spent most of her time in the country.

Six years after he came to the throne, Edward died from tuberculosis (a serious lung disease). Mary was crowned Queen Mary I of England shortly after this.

A Catholic queen

Queen Mary was determined to make England into a **Catholic** country once again. To help her in her task, she decided to marry a Catholic. Mary chose Philip, the only son of the King of Spain. This was a very unpopular choice. Many people feared that the Spanish prince would take control of England.

Protestant protest

The English **Protestants** hated the idea of a Catholic queen, and they wanted Elizabeth to rule instead. When Mary announced her plans to marry Philip of Spain, a Protestant **nobleman** led a **rebellion** against her. The rebellion failed and the nobleman was captured. He was later **executed**. But Mary was still angry. She thought Elizabeth had helped to plan the rebellion.

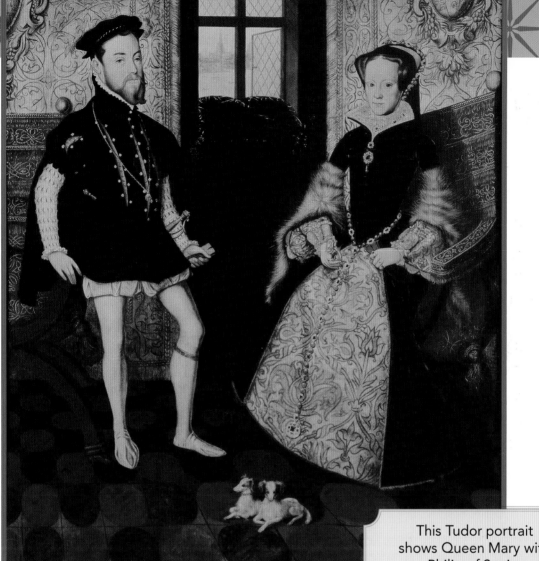

This Tudor portrait shows Queen Mary with Philip of Spain.

Spanish power

In Elizabeth's time, Spain was the richest and most powerful country in the world. The King of Spain ruled vast areas of land in South America. Ships full of silver and gold sailed from America to Spain.

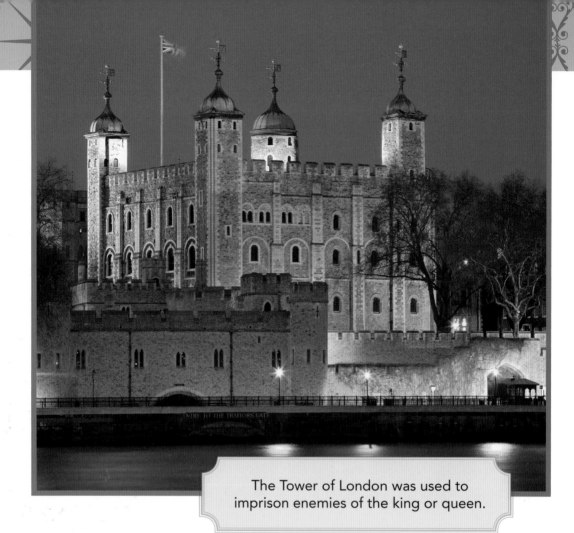

The Tower of London was used to imprison enemies of the king or queen.

Locked in the tower

Elizabeth told Mary that she knew nothing about the **rebellion**, but Mary wasn't taking any chances. She gave orders that Elizabeth should be locked in the Tower of London. The Tower was England's most terrifying prison. Most people who entered it never came out alive.

Elizabeth spent two months in the Tower before Mary decided to set her free. Then she was taken to a small palace near Oxford. Mary insisted that Elizabeth should stay in the palace for the next year.

A troubled reign

Queen Mary had a short and troubled **reign**. Even though she married Prince Philip of Spain, they did not have any children. She also failed to turn England into a **Catholic** country. In 1558, Mary died and Philip returned to Spain. Now it was Elizabeth's turn to rule.

Elizabeth is queen

Elizabeth was at Hatfield House when she heard the news that her sister had died and she was queen. She set off on a grand procession to London, and was welcomed by cheering crowds. But not everyone was pleased that she was queen. There were many challenges ahead.

When Mary (below) was queen she imprisoned her sister Elizabeth because she feared a rebellion.

Elizabeth's words, when she heard the news that she was queen of England.

"This is God's doing; it is marvellous in our eyes."

THE NEW QUEEN

Elizabeth was crowned Queen Elizabeth I of England in January 1559. The day before her **coronation** she was carried through the streets of London in an open carriage.

After she had been crowned, a very grand feast was held in her honour. It was a dramatic start to the young queen's **reign**.

This painting shows Elizabeth in her coronation robes.

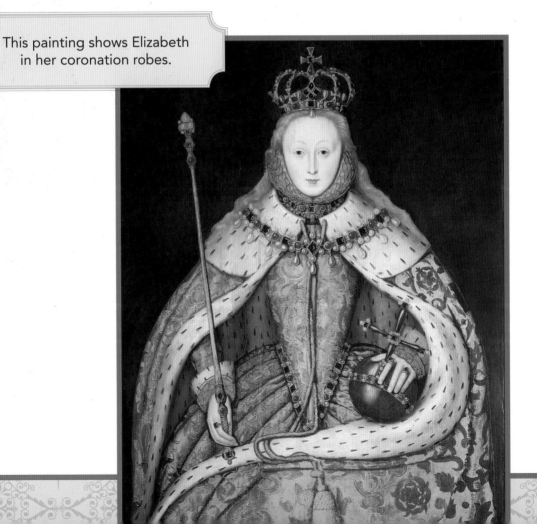

Elizabeth in charge

At first, people worried that a young woman of 25 could not rule England on her own. But Elizabeth soon showed that she was in charge. At the first meeting of her **advisors**, she announced that she expected all her people to obey her.

Elizabeth also insisted that everyone at the royal **court** show her great respect. No one was allowed to sit when she was standing. Anyone who spoke to the queen had to kneel on one knee.

Taking advice

Elizabeth held meetings with her advisors every day. She also took the advice of **Parliament**. This was a group of men who had been chosen to represent the English people. Elizabeth was very intelligent and she enjoyed the challenge of ruling well.

Sir William Cecil was Elizabeth's chief advisor. He served the queen for 40 years.

Only the best

Elizabeth liked to be surrounded by good-looking people. There is a story that she once refused to employ a young man because he had a front tooth missing!

Many homes

As queen, Elizabeth owned many palaces and homes. In winter she spent most of her time in Whitehall Palace in London. In summer she visited her country homes. One of her favourite homes was Hampton Court Palace. The palace was about 16 kilometres (10 miles) from the centre of London, on the bank of the River Thames.

Elizabeth's court

Wherever she travelled, Elizabeth was surrounded by her royal **court**. The court was made up partly of Elizabeth's friends, **advisors**, and servants. All these people were known as the queen's **courtiers**.

Elizabeth's father, King Henry VIII, rebuilt Hampton Court Palace.

Elizabeth was carried in an open carriage, surrounded by servants.

Many others came to court just to see the queen. Sometimes as many as 10,000 people gathered in the royal palaces for a special event such as a dance.

Royal tours

Elizabeth knew that it was very important to be seen by her people. She made special journeys all over England. She was carried in an open carriage at the head of a grand procession. Behind the queen came her courtiers, riding on horseback, and her servants, walking on foot. They were followed by many covered wagons filled with Elizabeth's dresses and jewellery.

Entertaining the Queen

When Queen Elizabeth toured her kingdom, she usually stayed the night with a **noble** family. It was very expensive having the Queen to stay. The families who welcomed Elizabeth had to look after all her courtiers and servants as well. Often there were 1,000 people to feed.

A husband for the queen?

Everyone at **court** expected Elizabeth to marry. Even though she was a strong ruler, people still thought she needed a husband. They also thought the queen should have children, to provide an **heir** to the throne. But Elizabeth was not in a hurry to find a husband.

When Elizabeth was asked in **Parliament** when she was going to marry, she replied:

"I am already bound unto a husband, which is the kingdom of England."

Foreign suitors

Many powerful men offered to marry Elizabeth. She had offers of marriage from Philip of Spain and from royal princes in Sweden and France.

Elizabeth took her time to respond to these offers. She had to decide if she really wanted England to be linked to another country. For a long time, she kept her admirers guessing. Then she refused them all.

Sweet Robin

Elizabeth was very fond of an English **nobleman** called Robert Dudley. She had known Dudley since she was eight, and she sometimes called him "sweet Robin". But Dudley had a wife, so he could not marry the queen.

Some people think that Elizabeth never married because she was in love with Robert Dudley. Others think she made a choice to stay single. They believe Elizabeth got used to ruling alone, and she did not want to share her power.

Elizabeth and Dudley liked
to play music together.

PLOTS AGAINST THE QUEEN

As soon as Elizabeth became queen, she announced that England was a **Protestant** country. This made the English **Catholics** very unhappy. Some of them even wanted to kill Elizabeth and replace her with a Catholic ruler.

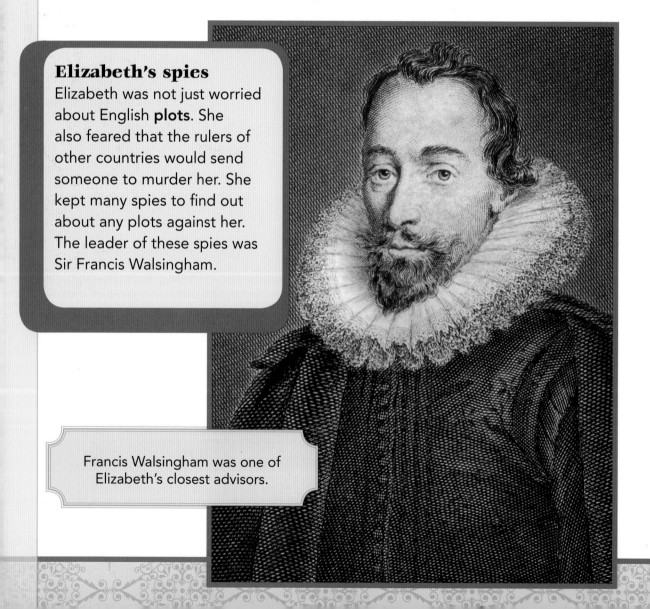

Elizabeth's spies

Elizabeth was not just worried about English **plots**. She also feared that the rulers of other countries would send someone to murder her. She kept many spies to find out about any plots against her. The leader of these spies was Sir Francis Walsingham.

Francis Walsingham was one of Elizabeth's closest advisors.

Mary Stuart, Queen of Scots

Many English Catholics wanted Mary Stuart (often called Mary Queen of Scots) to be their queen. Mary was Elizabeth's cousin, and a Catholic. For a while, she was queen of Scotland. But then the Scots turned against her because they did not trust the man she had married. They made her son, James, the new Scottish king, and captured Mary.

Mary was kept a prisoner in English castles for 19 years.

Mary in England

In 1568, Mary escaped to England and asked Elizabeth to protect her. This put Elizabeth in a very difficult situation. She was afraid that if Mary lived freely in England, she could lead a Catholic **rebellion** and try to replace Elizabeth as queen.

Elizabeth decided it was far too dangerous for her cousin Mary to be free. She gave orders that Mary should be kept as a prisoner. Elizabeth also made sure that Mary lived in comfort, however, with servants to look after her.

Early plots

Soon after Mary Stuart arrived in England, there were two attempts to make her queen. In 1569, some **Catholic noblemen** in the north of England led a **rebellion** against Elizabeth. They claimed that Mary was the true queen of England, but their rebellion was soon defeated.

Two years later, another Catholic nobleman tried to free Mary from prison. He was captured and **executed**, but Elizabeth did not have Mary killed. There was no proof that Mary knew about the **plot**, so Elizabeth refused to punish her.

The Babington plot

In 1586, Mary was finally caught plotting against Elizabeth. The plot was organized by an English nobleman, Sir Anthony Babington. It also involved King Philip of Spain. This time Elizabeth realized she would have to take firm action.

Mary's death

Elizabeth was very unhappy about putting Mary to death, but **Parliament** persuaded her it had to be done. In 1587, she gave orders for Mary to be executed. Six months after the execution, Elizabeth ordered a grand funeral for her cousin. She wanted to show proper respect to another queen.

MARIA
D   G
SCOTIÆ
PIISSIMA REGINA
FRANCIÆ DOTARIA
ANNO
ÆTATIS REGNIQ
36
ANGLICÆ CAPTIVIT
10
S   H
1578

This portrait shows Mary Queen of Scots when she was around 35 years old. Mary was executed ten years after this, in 1587.

A hard decision

The day that Mary died, Elizabeth refused to see anyone and sent away her food. She would not even talk to her trusted **advisor**, Sir William Cecil. Elizabeth hated the thought of a queen being executed. It reminded her too much of her father's **reign**, when two queens (including Elizabeth's mother) were executed.

ELIZABETH AT WAR

Elizabeth's great enemy was King Philip of Spain. Philip was a **devout Catholic** who hated the fact that England was a **Protestant** country. He also had other reasons for hating Elizabeth.

Raids at sea

Spain owned vast areas of land in South America. This meant that many Spanish ships crossed the Atlantic Ocean, sailing from South America to Spain. The ships were filled with treasure such as silver and gold. Elizabeth saw the chance to steal this treasure for England.

Elizabeth sent daring sea captains into the Atlantic to trade and explore. But the captains also attacked the Spanish ships and stole their treasure. When Philip protested about these attacks, Elizabeth said there was nothing she could do to stop them. This made Philip furious.

Philip and Elizabeth

Before he became king of Spain, Philip had been married to Elizabeth's half-sister Mary. When Mary died, Philip offered to marry Elizabeth, so he could keep control of England. Elizabeth refused Philip's offer of marriage, and gradually the two rulers became enemies.

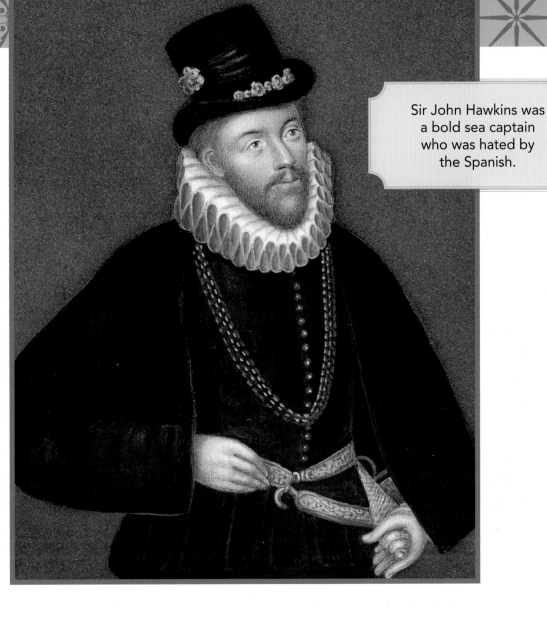

Sir John Hawkins was a bold sea captain who was hated by the Spanish.

Time to attack

In 1585, Elizabeth upset the Spanish again. She sent some English troops to support the Netherlands in their war against Spain. Two years later, Mary, Queen of Scots was **executed**. Philip was shocked at the death of a Catholic queen. He decided it was time to **invade** England.

Preparing for war

In 1588, about 130 ships set off from Spain. This massive **fleet** was known as the Spanish **Armada**. Meanwhile, Elizabeth prepared for war. She gathered an army at Tilbury, and a fleet of around 150 ships at Plymouth (see map on page 5). Then the English waited for the Spanish ships to arrive.

On 29 July, the Armada reached the French **port** of Calais. Here, the Spanish rested for the night before they crossed the English Channel to attack England. However, the English **navy** had another plan. They decided to surprise the Armada.

This portrait of Elizabeth shows the ships of the Armada behind her.

In this painting, the English fire ships are being sent towards the Spanish fleet.

Battle begins

At midnight, the English sent eight fire ships towards the Armada. Fire ships were empty wooden ships that had been set on fire. The blazing ships caused a lot of damage to the Armada. Several Spanish ships burst into flames.

Later, the two fleets fought a battle at sea. There was no clear winner, but the Armada was greatly weakened. Then a violent storm arrived. Powerful winds blew the Spanish ships out of the English Channel. England was now out of danger.

The end of the Armada

Driven by storms, the Armada was forced to sail all the way around the British Isles. Many Spanish ships were wrecked, and the remaining fleet returned to Spain. Elizabeth had won a victory against Spain.

Bowls or battle?

One of the leading captains of the English fleet was Sir Francis Drake. He always stayed very calm in battle. When the Armada was sighted, Drake was playing a game of **bowls**. He calmly finished the game before he returned to his ship.

Good Queen Bess

After the defeat of the Spanish **Armada**, people in England felt much safer than before. They felt very proud of their queen, and they gave her the name "Good Queen Bess". In the course of her long **reign**, Good Queen Bess made her country great in many ways.

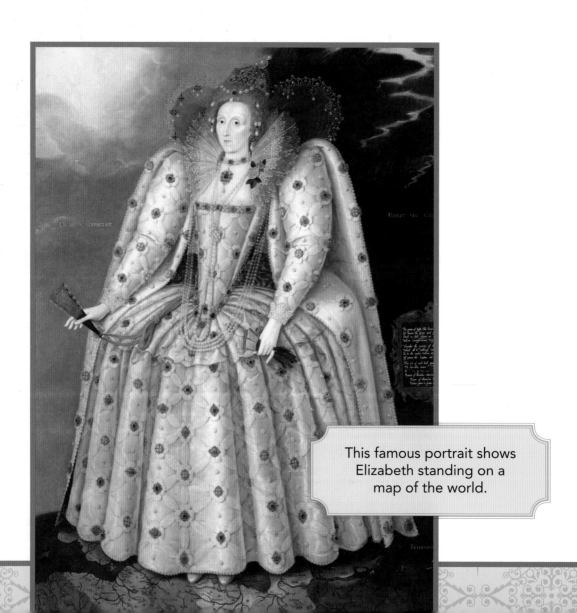

This famous portrait shows Elizabeth standing on a map of the world.

Sir Francis Drake had many adventures. He even explored the Antarctic Ocean.

Exploring the world

During Elizabeth's reign, England was famous for its explorers. The queen paid for many daring **voyages** to discover new land. Martin Frobisher reached northern Canada, and Humphrey Gilbert claimed Newfoundland for his queen.

Francis Drake was the most famous Elizabethan explorer. He sailed all the way round the world in his ship, the *Golden Hind*. When Drake returned, Elizabeth made him a knight, giving him the title "Sir Francis Drake".

Settling in America

Another explorer, Sir Walter Raleigh, made the first English voyage to America. He landed on the east coast of America and called the place where he landed "Virginia". The other people with Raleigh tried to live in Virginia for a while. However, they found the life very hard and they did not stay long.

Gifts from America

Sir Walter Raleigh was a great favourite of Elizabeth's. There is a famous story that he brought two gifts for her from America. According to the story, Raleigh presented Elizabeth with potatoes and tobacco. Nobody knows if this is true.

Shakespeare's plays were performed at the Globe Theatre in London.

Poetry and plays

Elizabeth was very proud of the talents of her people. She encouraged writers, artists, and musicians. Poets came to her **court** to read her their works. **Playwrights** performed their latest plays in front of the Queen.

The greatest writer of Elizabeth's time was William Shakespeare. It is believed that some of Shakespeare's plays were written especially to please the Queen.

Marvellous music

Queen Elizabeth was very musical. As well as singing and dancing she played the lute (a kind of early guitar). She also played the virginals (a keyboard instrument).

In Elizabeth's **reign**, **composers** wrote great music for church services. They also composed madrigals, which were songs with different parts for high and low voices.

Fantastic fashions

Elizabeth thought it was very important to dress magnificently. She also expected everyone else at court to dress well. Elizabeth had more than 250 dresses made from velvet, satin, and silk. She wore dazzling jewellery, and even had jewels and pearls in her hair.

Smart but smelly

People at Elizabeth's court dressed very fashionably, but they did not smell very nice. In Elizabethan times, even very wealthy people rarely took a bath, and their clothes were not often washed. Some people carried a fruit stuffed with **cloves**. They hoped the strong smell of the cloves would disguise the other smells!

At Elizabeth's court, musicians played while people ate.

Encouraging trade

Elizabeth recognized that trade was very important for her country. She encouraged **merchants** to find new markets for their goods. During her **reign**, English merchants began to trade in America. Traders also travelled to new areas of Africa and Asia. By the time Elizabeth died, England was a wealthy nation.

A growing city

The city of London grew very fast in Elizabethan times. London had some fine houses and gardens, but it also had many crowded buildings and narrow streets. The River Thames ran through the centre of London. London Bridge was the only crossing place, but there were many barges to carry people across the river.

St Paul's Church (at the top of this picture) was a famous landmark of the Elizabethan city of London.

Helping the poor

In Elizabeth's time, there was not enough food to feed everyone in England. Some people even starved to death. Elizabeth made the rich pay taxes (money for the government). She used this money to help support the poor and to build **workhouses**. Workhouses were places where very poor people could live and work.

Rich and poor

In Elizabethan times, the rich and poor had very different lives. Wealthy people lived in enormous homes with many servants. They ate at huge banquets and dressed in fine clothes. Poor people lived in very small cottages, or had no homes at all. Their main food was bread or porridge, and they wore simple clothes or rags. Many poor people had no proper shoes, even in winter.

Beggars and other poor people were a common sight in Elizabethan England. This beggar is being dragged through the streets.

THE END OF A GOLDEN AGE

Elizabeth ruled England until her death, at the age of 69. She stayed fairly fit, but the last years of her **reign** were hard for her. Most of her friends had died and she was very lonely.

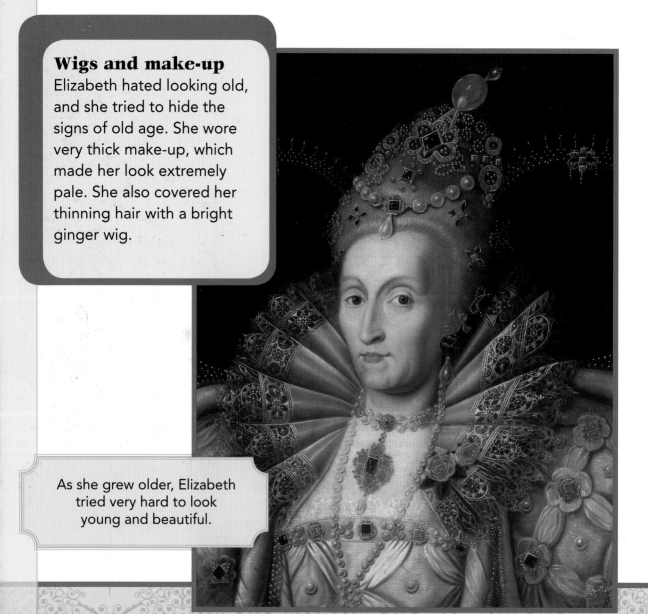

Wigs and make-up
Elizabeth hated looking old, and she tried to hide the signs of old age. She wore very thick make-up, which made her look extremely pale. She also covered her thinning hair with a bright ginger wig.

As she grew older, Elizabeth tried very hard to look young and beautiful.

Losing Dudley

As Elizabeth grew older, the person she missed most was Robert Dudley. He was probably her closest friend and she trusted his advice. Dudley died at the time of the Spanish **Armada**, when Elizabeth was around 55 years old. She never recovered from his death. She kept his last letter by her bed for the rest of her life.

Elizabeth and Essex

In the last years of her reign, Elizabeth spent a lot of time with a handsome young **nobleman**, known as the Earl of Essex.

Elizabeth gave the Earl of Essex a lot of power, but that just made him hungry for more. Around 1600 he led a **rebellion** against the queen. The rebellion was a failure and Essex was **executed**. Elizabeth was very sad that her favourite had turned against her. Now she felt even more alone.

The Earl of Essex was young, and greedy for power.

Death of a queen

In her final years, Elizabeth often suffered from toothache, but she refused to have her teeth pulled out. She also started to go blind and her memory began to fail.

In February 1603 Elizabeth caught a fever, and a few weeks later she died. She was given a magnificent funeral at Westminster Abbey in London.

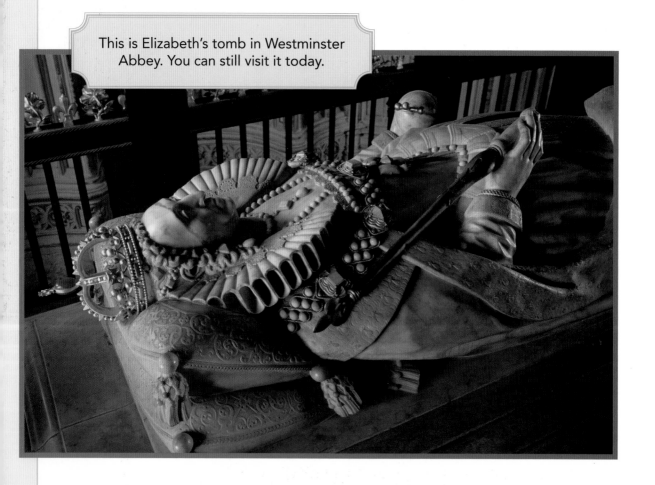

This is Elizabeth's tomb in Westminster Abbey. You can still visit it today.

Who will be next?

Because Elizabeth had no children, she had to choose England's next ruler. But she always refused to name her **successor**. Finally, she chose King James VI of Scotland. James was the son of Mary Queen of Scots. He was a **Protestant** and a member of the Stuart family.

James was crowned King James I of England. The **reign** of the Tudor family had come to an end, and a new line of Stuart rulers had begun.

A golden age

After Elizabeth's death, people saw her reign as a "golden age". They recognized all the things she had done to make her country great. In her long reign, Elizabeth had proved that a woman could be a strong and **inspiring** leader.

James I was the new king of England.

Throughout her life, Elizabeth was keen to show that women could be just as good as men. At the time of the Spanish **Armada**, she told her army:

"I have but the body of a weak and feeble woman, but I have the heart and stomach of a king."

TIMELINES

Elizabeth's life

1533   Elizabeth is born

1536   Anne Boleyn (Elizabeth's mother) is **executed**

1547   King Henry VIII dies. Edward VI becomes king.

1553   King Edward VI dies. Lady Jane Grey **reigns** for just nine days. Mary I becomes queen.

1554   A Protestant nobleman called Sir Thomas Wyatt leads a **rebellion** against Queen Mary

1558   Queen Mary I dies. Elizabeth I becomes queen.

1568   Elizabeth imprisons Mary Queen of Scots

1569   The first **Protestant** rebellion against Elizabeth is defeated

1580   Sir Francis Drake returns from his **voyage** around the world

1584   Sir Walter Raleigh claims Virginia, in North America, for Elizabeth

1585   Elizabeth sends troops to support the Netherlands in a war against Spain

1586   The Babington **plot** against Elizabeth is discovered

1587   Mary Queen of Scots is executed

1588   The Spanish **Armada** is defeated. Robert Dudley dies.

1598   William Cecil dies

1601   The Earl of Essex is executed, after his rebellion against the Queen fails

1603   Queen Elizabeth I dies. James I becomes king.

World timeline

1521   Spanish troops **conquer** the Aztec people and take control of Mexico

1526   Babur becomes the first Mughal Emperor of India

1535   Spanish troops conquer the Inca Empire and take control of Peru, in South America

1543   Andreas Vesalius, from Brussels, is the first person to make a detailed study of the human body

1547   Tsar Ivan IV (known as Ivan the Terrible) starts to rule in Russia

1562   England joins the slave trade, shipping slaves from Africa to America

1564   William Shakespeare is born

1566   The Turkish Ottoman Empire reaches its largest size

1600   The East India Company is created in England, to trade with India

1600   The Oyo kingdom in West Africa is at its height

GLOSSARY

advisor someone who gives helpful advice. Elizabeth had many advisors who helped her to make some difficult decisions.

armada very large number of ships. The Spanish Armada included around 150 ships.

astronomer someone who studies the stars and the planets. Galileo was a famous astronomer.

bowls game played with large, heavy balls on a flat grassy surface

Catholic someone who belongs to a branch of the Christian Church that is led by the pope in Rome. Catholics are sometimes also known as Roman Catholics.

Church of England branch of the Christian religion. The Church of England is sometimes called the Anglican Church.

cloves dried, unopened buds of the clove tree, which are used as a strong-smelling spice

composer someone who writes music. Beethoven was a famous composer.

conquer defeat an enemy and take control of them by force

coronation religious service, in which a new king or queen is crowned. Elizabeth I's coronation was held in 1558.

court people who gather around a ruler, including their advisors and servants. The court usually gathers in a royal palace.

courtier someone who is close to a ruler, and is an important figure at the royal court. Queen Elizabeth I liked to be surrounded by courtiers.

devout very keen on religion. Devout Christians spend a lot of time praying and going to church.

divorce legal end of a marriage

execute kill someone as punishment for a crime. In the world today, very few people are executed.

fleet large number of ships. A fleet is usually smaller than an armada.

governess woman who teaches children in their own home. Today, it is very unusual for children to have a governess.

heir person who will receive money, land, or a job when his or her parents die. When Queen Elizabeth II dies, Prince Charles will become king because he is the heir to the British throne.

inspire encourage another person to do something by setting a good example. Football stars inspire young players to practise harder.

invade send soldiers into another country in order to take it over

lady-in-waiting woman who helps to look after a queen. Queen Elizabeth I had ladies-in-waiting to help her put on her clothes and arrange her hair.

merchant someone who trades with foreign countries. In Tudor times, merchants travelled long distances by ship.

monastery group of buildings where monks live and work. Buddhists, Hindus, and Christians have monasteries.

navy ships and sailors that fight for a country at sea. In Tudor times England had a powerful navy.

noble person who has a very high rank in society. Lords and ladies are nobles.

parliament group of people who make the laws of the country. Members of parliament represent the people, and are voted for in an election.

playwright someone who writes plays. William Shakespeare is one of the world's most famous playwrights.

plot secret plan. Sometimes people make plots to kill an enemy.

pope leader of the Catholic Church. The pope lives in Rome.

port town with a harbour. Ships stop in ports to unload their goods and passengers.

Protestant someone who belongs to a branch of the Christian Church that does not have the pope as its leader. Protestants broke away from the Catholic Church in the 1500s.

rebellion violent protest against a ruler or a government. There were three major rebellions during Elizabeth's reign.

reign period of time that a king or queen rules for. The reign of Queen Elizabeth I lasted for 45 years.

successor person who takes over a job when somebody dies or stops working

voyage journey by sea. You can go on a voyage on a sailing boat or on an ocean liner.

workhouse place where poor people worked in return for food and shelter. There were workhouses in Britain until the 1800s.

WANT TO KNOW MORE?

Books

British History Makers: Queen Elizabeth I, Leon Ashworth, (Cherrytree Books, 2002)

Focus on Tudor Life: Elizabeth I, Liz Gogerly, (Franklin Watts, 2006)

Good Queen Bess: The Story of Elizabeth I of England Diane Stanley and Peter Vennema (Harper Collins, 2001)

Horribly Famous: Elizabeth I and her conquests, Margaret Simpson and Philip Reeve (Scholastic, 2006)

Websites

http://tudorhistory.org/elizabeth/
This site has a biography of Elizabeth, illustrated with lots of paintings.

http://www.bbc.co.uk/history/historic_figures/elizabeth_i_queen.shtml
This site covers many aspects of Elizabeth's reign. It includes a spying game and a view inside an Elizabethan room.

http://www.tudorbritain.org/
A fun site about Tudor life with lots of activities.

Places to visit

Fotheringhay Castle, Peterborough, Northamptonshire
The place where Mary Queen of Scots was executed.

Hatfield House, Hertfordshire
Elizabeth's childhood home.

Westminster Abbey, London
Tombs of Elizabeth I and Mary Queen of Scots.

Tower of London, London
The prison where the young Elizabeth was held.

National Portrait Gallery, London
This gallery contains many portraits of famous Tudors.

INDEX